Okay-okay! We know you're eager to start learning but first let us instruct you on

HOW TO USE THIS BOOK

This book is splitted into 5 chapters:

1. Cursive Handwriting Crash Course

If you are completely new to cursive handwriting this section will jump-start your learning process. Start with the basic strokes and learn how to write various letters that are based on them starting with lowercase letters and then moving on to uppercase ones. As soon as you know how to write your first letters you can start practicing writing words with them. At the end of the chapter you can practice writing some pangrams (sentences that contain all the letters of the alphabet).

2. Letters Writing Practice

In this chapter you will practice writing lowercase and uppercase letters. Since cursive writing is all about connections, each letter of the alphabet in its uppercase form and its connections with all the letters of the alphabet in lowercase form will be represented on a separate page. Please feel free to copy these pages to get more resources for practicing.

3. Alternative Capital Letters

Cursive handwriting is a dynamic process. Letter forms change over time. Some people prefer some forms over the others. In this chapter we provide several uppercase letters in their alternative forms.

4. Sentences Writing Practice

In this chapter you will practice writing sentences each of which focuses on a particular letter of the alphabet.

5. Blank Writing Practice Sheets

Here you will have some space to write your own words and sentences using the skills that you have learnt with this book.

Let's start learning!

We are happy to receive any of your feedback regarding this workbook at:
lilas.publishing@ya.ru

Lilas Lingvo Team

Contents

Cursive Handwriting Crash Course **5**

Lesson 1: Wave strokes..7
Lesson 2: Letters 'i', 's', 'r' and 't'..8
Lesson 3: Words with letters 'i', 's', 'r' and 't' 10
Lesson 4: Short curved wave stroke 12
Lesson 5: Letters 'a', 'o', 'd', 'g' and 'c'...12
Lesson 6: Words with letters 'a', 'o', 'd', 'g' and 'c' 16
Lesson 7: Cursive hill stroke 19
Lesson 8: Letters 'm' and 'n'...19
Lesson 9: Words with letters 'm' and 'n' 21
Lesson 10: Letters 'u' and 'w'...22
Lesson 11: Words with letters 'u' and 'w' 23
Lesson 12: Short loop and long loop strokes...25
Lesson 13: Letters 'e', 'l' and 'b'..26
Lesson 14: Words with letters 'e', 'l' and 'b'...28
Lesson 15: Letters 'k', 'h' and 'f'..31
Lesson 16: Words with letters 'k', 'h' and 'f' 33
Lesson 17: Letter 'q'...35
Lesson 18: Words with the letter 'q'...35
Lesson 19: Short wave loop stroke..37
Lesson 20: Letters 'j', 'p' and 'y' 38
Lesson 21: Words with letters 'j', 'p' and 'y' 40
Lesson 22: Letters 'z', 'v' and 'x' 42
Lesson 23: Words with letters 'z', 'v' and 'x' 44
Lesson 24: Long curved wave stroke 46
Lesson 25: Uppercase letters 'C', 'A' and 'O'..46
Lesson 26: Words with letters 'C', 'A' and 'O'.......................................47
Lesson 27: Long wave stroke..50
Lesson 28: Uppercase letters 'U', 'Y' and 'V'...50
Lesson 29: Words with letters 'U', 'Y' and 'V' 51
Lesson 30: Uppercase letters 'T', 'F' and 'S' 54
Lesson 31: Words with uppercase letters 'T', 'F' and 'S'......................55
Lesson 32: Cursive long hill stroke..57
Lesson 33: Uppercase letters 'H', 'K', 'M' and 'N'................................57
Lesson 34: Words with uppercase letters 'H', 'K', 'M' and 'N' 59

Lesson 35: Uppercase letters 'B', 'P', and 'R' 62
Lesson 36: Words with uppercase letters 'B', 'P', and 'R' 63
Lesson 37: Uppercase letters 'G', 'L', and 'Q' 65
Lesson 38: Words with uppercase letters 'G', 'L', and 'Q' 66
Lesson 39: Uppercase letters 'D', 'E', and 'Z' 68
Lesson 40: Words with uppercase letters 'D', 'E', and 'Z' 69
Lesson 41: Uppercase letters 'I' and 'J' 71
Lesson 42: Words with uppercase letters 'I' and 'J' 72
Lesson 43: Uppercase letters 'W' and 'X' 73
Lesson 44: Words with uppercase letters 'W' and 'X' 74
Lesson 45: Numbers writing practice 75
Lesson 46: Pangram writing practice 79

Letters Writing Practice **83**

Alternative Capital Letters **111**

Sentences Writing Practice **121**

Blank Writing Practice Sheets **135**

Cursive Handwriting Crash Course

Lesson 1: Wave strokes

There are a variety of approaches to learning how to write cursive. We will try not to over complicate matters in this course and quickly start your cursive handwriting right away.

In the first lesson you will practice writing 'wave' strokes (thus called as they resemble little waves). First let's try writing short wave strokes.

Now let's write tall wave strokes.

Lesson 2: Letters 'i', 's', 'r' and 't'

In this lesson you will learn how to turn short and long wave strokes into letters 'i', 's', 'r' and 't'. Let's start with 'i'.

Make your short wave stroke and then dot each spike:

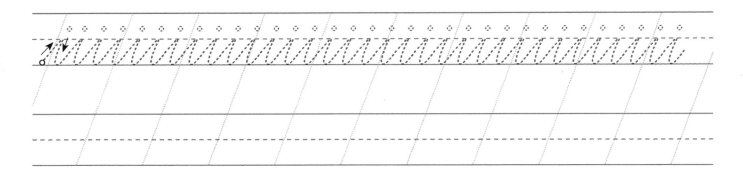

Now let's write the letter 'i' separately. Start a short wave stroke and stop between the bottom line and the middle line. Dot the spikes:

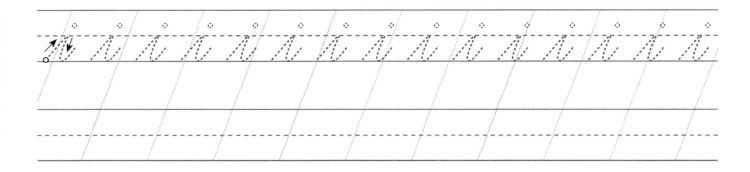

Now we'll turn a short wave stroke into the letter 's'. Start a short wave stroke, open it up, bring it up to almost touch the wave, then pull it back up and start again:

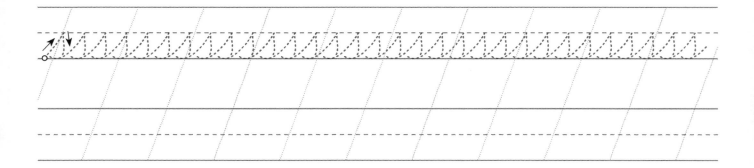

8

Now let's write the letter 's' separately. Start a short wave stroke, open it up, almost touch the wave, pull it back up, give it a little tail and stop:

Now we'll turn a short wave stroke into the letter 'r'. Start a short wave stroke, stop at the middle line, make a little curve, bring it down and then pull back up to the middle line:

Now let's write the letter 'r' separately. Start a short wave stroke, stop at the middle line, make a little curve, bring it down, then stop half way between the bottom and the middle lines:

Now we are going to use a long wave stroke to write the letter 't'. Make a long wave stroke almost to the top line, then cross the tall spikes right on the middle line:

Now let's write the letter 't' separately. Make a long wave stroke almost to the top line, pull it down, stop between the bottom line and the middle line, then cross the spike right on the middle line:

Lesson 3: Words with letters 'i', 's', 'r' and 't'

In this lesson you will practice writing words with cursive using the letters that you've learnt. Practice writing these words until you'll get comfortable writing them:

its its its its its its its

its its its its its its its

stir stir stir stir stir stir

stir stir stir stir stir stir

sir sir sir sir sir sir sir

sir sir sir sir sir sir sir

Lesson 4: Short curved wave stroke

In this lesson you will learn how to write a short curved wave stroke. It is similar to the short wave stroke that we've learnt only there is a small curve at the top of it.

Lesson 5: Letters 'a', 'o', 'd', 'g' and 'c'

In this lesson you will learn how to write letters 'a', 'o', 'd', 'g' and 'c' using a short curved wave stroke.

Let's start with the letter 'a'. Make a curved wave stroke as usual only at the end bring the bottom stroke up to touch the tip of the curved wave and then pull back down:

Now let's write the letter 'a' separately. Make a curved wave stroke, bring the bottom stroke up to touch the tip of curve and give it a little tail:

Now we'll turn a curved wave stroke into the letter 'o'. Make a curved wave stroke, bring the bottom stroke up to touch the tip of the curve, make a little loop at the top of the letter and give it a little link from there:

Now let's write the letter 'o' separately. Make a curved wave stroke, bring the bottom stroke up to touch the tip of the curve, make a little loop at the top of the letter and give it a little link from there:

Now we're going to write the letter 'd' using the curved wave stroke. Make a curved wave stroke, bring the bottom stroke up, touch the tip of the top curve, bring the stroke almost all the way up to the top line, then bring it down and start all over again:

Now let's write the letter 'd' separately. Make a curved wave stroke, bring the bottom stroke up to the tip of the top curve, then all the way up to the top line, then down and give it a little tail:

Now we'll turn a curved wave stroke into the letter 'g'. Make a curved wave stroke, bring the bottom stroke up to touch the tip of the curve, then bring it down below the bottom line and make a loop and then go up:

Now let's write the letter 'g' separately. Make a curved wave stroke, bring the bottom stroke up to touch the tip of the curve, then bring it down below the bottom line and make a loop and go up:

Now we'll turn a curved wave stroke into the letter 'c'. It is just the same as the curved wave stroke itself. When you're making a curved wave stroke you're making the letter 'c':

Now let's write the letter 'c' separately. Make a curved wave stroke, pull it up halfway between the bottom line and the middle line and stop:

Lesson 6: Words with letters 'a', 'o', 'd', 'g' and 'c'

In this lesson you will practice writing words with cursive using the letters that you've learnt so far. Practice writing these words until you'll get comfortable writing them:

coat coat coat coat coat

coat coat coat coat coat

cod cod cod cod cod cod

cod cod cod cod cod cod

nag nag nag nag nag nag

nag nag nag nag nag nag

door door door door door

door door door door door

got got got got got got

got got got got got got

road road road road

road road road road

Lesson 7: Cursive hill stroke

In this lesson we are going to practice the 'cursive hill stroke'. Make sure that the top of the 'hill' touches the middle line:

Lesson 8: Letters 'm' and 'n'

In this lesson you will be turning the hill stroke into the letters 'm' and 'n'. Let's start with 'm'. First create a little tail, make two hill strokes, then pull the stroke up and start again:

Now let's write the letter 'm' separately. Start with a little tail, make two hill strokes and then finish with a little tail:

Writing the letter 'n' is very similar to 'm'. Start with a little tail, make one hill stroke, then pull the stroke back up and start again:

Now let's write the letter 'n' separately. Start with a little tail, make one hill stroke and then finish with a little tail:

Lesson 9: Words with letters 'm' and 'n'

In this lesson you will practice writing words using letters and strokes that you've learnt so far. Practice writing these words until you'll get comfortable writing them:

man man man man

man man man man

moon moon moon moon

moon moon moon moon

moon moon moon

moon moon moon

moan moan moan

moan moan moan

Lesson 10: Letters 'u' and 'w'

In this lesson we are going to use the short wave stroke again to practice writing letters 'u' and 'w'. Let's start with 'u'. Make a short wave stroke, make a connection and start again:

Now let's write the letter 'u' separately. Make a short wave stroke, then another short wave stroke and then end it:

Now we are going to use the short wave stroke to write the letter 'w'. Make three short wave strokes and the add a little link to the next letter:

Now let's write the letter 'w' separately. Make three short wave strokes and then leave a little curve as the tail:

Lesson 11: Words with letters 'u' and 'w'

In this lesson we are going to use the short wave stroke again to practice writing letters 'u' and 'w'. Let's start with 'u'. Make a short wave stroke, then stretch the next stroke a little further and then start again:

mag mag mag mag

mag mag mag mag mag

mag mag mag mag mag

strain strain strain strain

strain strain strain strain

us us us us us us us us

Lesson 12: Short loop and long loop strokes

In this lesson you will learn two new strokes: the short loop stroke and the long loop stroke. Let's start with the short loop. Start at the bottom line and make even loops that reach the middle line:

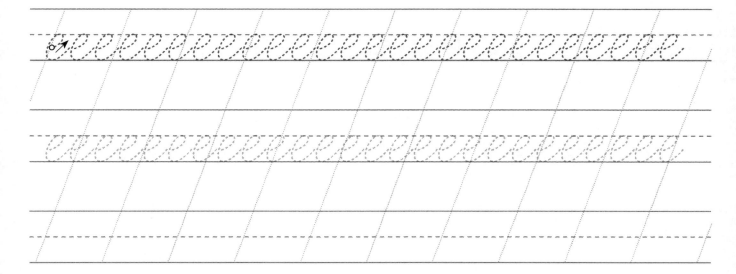

The tall loop is similar, only you pull the stroke all the way to the top line. Try to make straight nice looking loops:

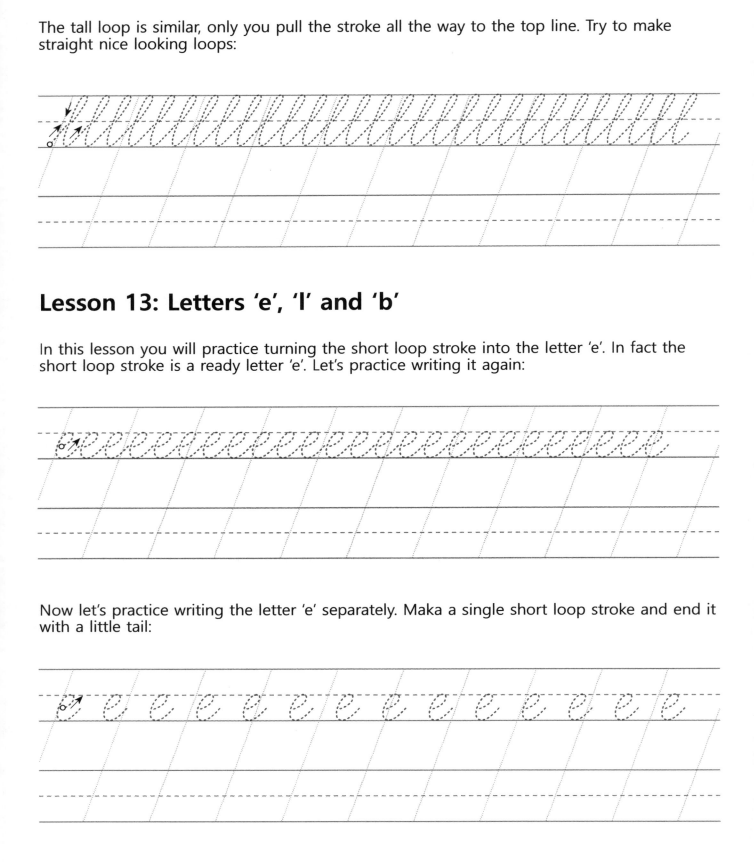

Lesson 13: Letters 'e', 'l' and 'b'

In this lesson you will practice turning the short loop stroke into the letter 'e'. In fact the short loop stroke is a ready letter 'e'. Let's practice writing it again:

Now let's practice writing the letter 'e' separately. Maka a single short loop stroke and end it with a little tail:

Now we are going to use the long loop stroke to create the letter 'l'. The way to do it is just writing long loop strokes:

Now let's practice writing the letter 'l' separately. Make a single long loop stroke and end it with a little tail:

Now we are going to use the long loop stroke to create the letter 'b'. First make a long loop stroke as usual, pull it up to the middle line, make a small loop, then pull the stoke to the right and start a new long loop stroke:

Now let's practice writing the letter 'b' separately. Make a long loop stroke, pull it up to the middle line, make a small loop, then pull to the right:

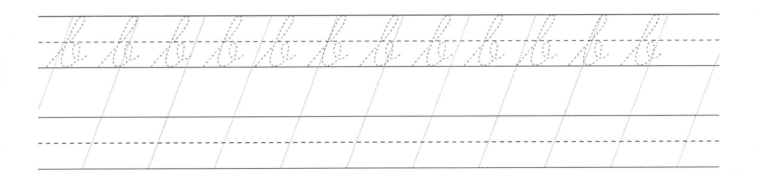

Lesson 14: Words with letters 'e', 'l' and 'b'

In this lesson you will practice writing words using letters and strokes that you've learnt so far. Practice writing these words until you'll get comfortable writing them:

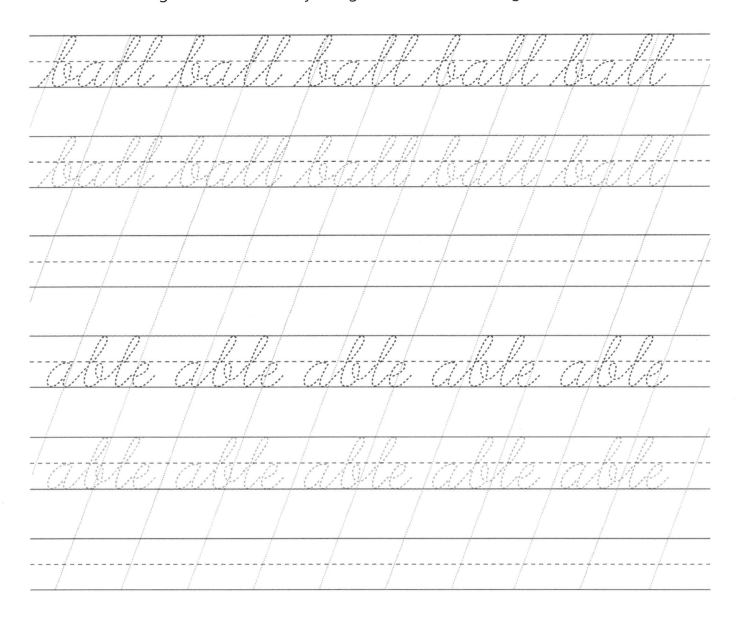

bleed bleed bleed bleed

bleed bleed bleed bleed

alone alone alone alone

alone alone alone alone

secure secure secure secure

secure secure secure secure

babble babble babble

babble babble babble

lonesome lonesome

lonesome lonesome

lecture lecture lecture

lecture lecture lecture

Lesson 15: Letters 'k', 'h' and 'f'

In this lesson you will be turning the long loop stroke into the letters 'k', 'h' and 'f'. Let's start with 'k'. Make a long loop stroke, stop at the bottom line, come back up to the middle line with a little arch, make a little loop there and then pull the stroke out:

Now let's practice writing the letter 'k' separately. Make a long loop stroke, stop at the bottom line, come back up to the middle line with a little arch, make a little loop and then pull the stroke out:

Now let's turn the long loop stroke into the letter 'h'. Make a long loop stroke, stop at the bottom and then make a hill. Come back up, make another loop and make a hill again:

Now let's practice writing the letter 'h' separately. Make a long loop stroke, stop at the bottom and then make a hill. End with a little tail:

Now we'll use the long loop stroke to make the letter 'f'. Start a long loop stroke and when you come down go below the bottom line, make a loop at the bottom touching the stroke where it crosses the bottom line and then start a new long loop stroke:

Now let's practice writing the letter 'f' separately. Start a long loop stroke and when you come down go below the bottom line, make a loop at the bottom and then end with a little tail:

Lesson 16: Words with letters 'k', 'h' and 'f'

In this lesson you will practice writing words using letters and strokes that you've learnt so far. Practice writing these words until you'll get comfortable writing them:

flock flock flock flock

flock flock flock flock

knock knock knock

knock knock knock

bleak bleak bleak bleak

bleak bleak bleak bleak

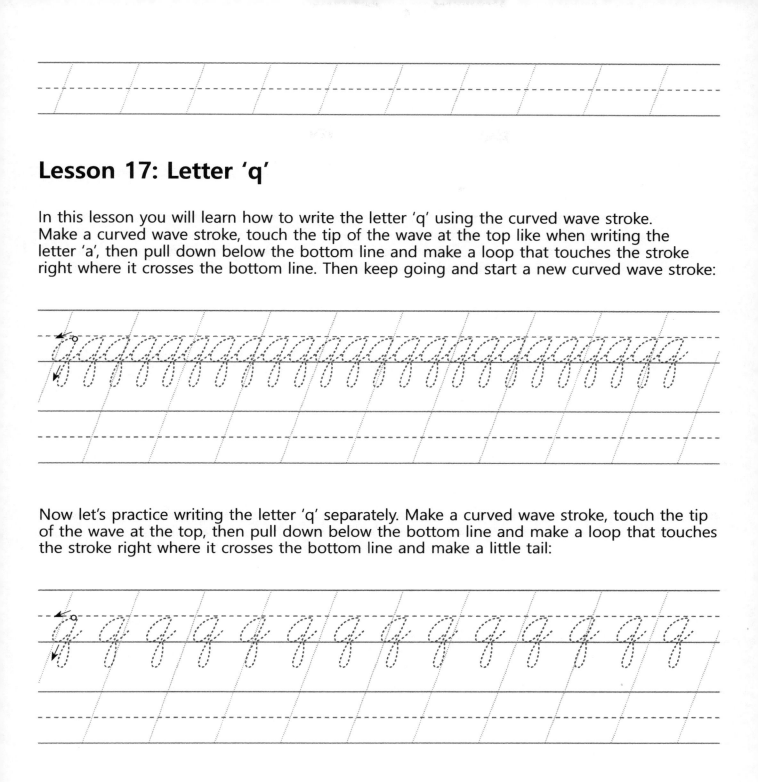

Lesson 17: Letter 'q'

In this lesson you will learn how to write the letter 'q' using the curved wave stroke. Make a curved wave stroke, touch the tip of the wave at the top like when writing the letter 'a', then pull down below the bottom line and make a loop that touches the stroke right where it crosses the bottom line. Then keep going and start a new curved wave stroke:

Now let's practice writing the letter 'q' separately. Make a curved wave stroke, touch the tip of the wave at the top, then pull down below the bottom line and make a loop that touches the stroke right where it crosses the bottom line and make a little tail:

Lesson 18: Words with the letter 'q'

In this lesson you will practice writing words using letters and strokes that you've learnt so far. Practice writing these words until you'll get comfortable writing them:

quit quit quit quit quit

quit quit quit quit quit

aqua aqua aqua aqua

aqua aqua aqua aqua

quake quake quake quake

quake quake quake quake

Lesson 19: Short wave loop stroke

In this lesson you will learn how to write the 'short wave loop stroke'. Start writing the short wave stroke. When you reach the middle line pull it down below the bottom line and make a loop to the left. Pull the stroke back up and cross the stroke at the bottom line:

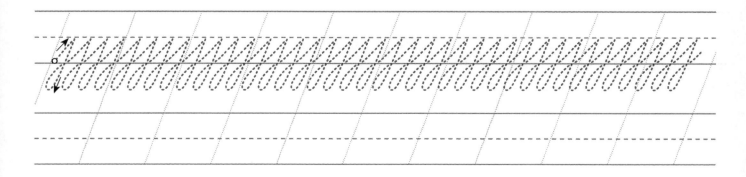

Lesson 20: Letters 'j', 'p' and 'y'

In this lesson you will be using the short wave loop stroke to write the letters 'j', 'p' and 'y'. Let's start with 'j'. Simply make the short wave loop stroke and then put the dots above the spikes:

Now let's practice writing the letter 'j' separately. Make a short wave loop stroke and when you pull the stroke above the bottom line end it with a little tail:

Now let's use the short wave loop stroke to write the letter 'p'. Make a short wave loop stroke only instead of making a loop below the bottom line, pull the stroke straight back up, make a loop between the bottom line and the middle line, pull the stroke right and start again:

Now let's practice writing the letter 'p' separately. Start a short wave loop stroke, pull it straight back up, make a loop between the bottom line and the middle line and pull a little tail to the right:

Now let's use the short wave loop stroke to write the letter 'y'. We start the letter 'y' with a short wave stroke and then a short wave loop stroke. Cross the stroke at the bottom line:

Now let's practice writing the letter 'y' separately. Start with a short wave stroke, then a short wave loop stroke. Cross the stroke at the bottom line and end with a little tail:

Lesson 21: Words with letters 'j', 'p' and 'y'

In this lesson you will practice writing words using letters and strokes that you've learnt so far. Practice writing these words until you'll get comfortable writing them:

pyjamas pyjamas

pyjamas pyjamas

jeepney jeepney jeepney

jeepney jeepney jeepney

popinjay popinjay

popinjay popinjay

Lesson 22: Letters 'z', 'v' and 'x'

In this lesson you will learn how to write the cursive letters 'z', 'v' and 'x'. Let's start with the letter 'z'. Make a hill stroke, then pull the stroke below the bottom line and make a loop there crossing the initial stroke at the bottom line:

Now let's practice writing the letter 'z' separately. Make a hill stroke then pull the stroke below the bottom line and make a loop there crossing the initial stroke at the bottom line:

Now we'll learn how to write the letter 'v'. Start with a little hill, make a curve at the bottom line, come back up and finish with a little tail. Letter 'v' is somewhat similar to the letter 'o' only with a gap at the top:

Now let's practice writing the letter 'v' separately. Start with a little hill, make a curve at the bottom line, come back up and finish with a little tail:

Now we'll learn how to write the letter 'x'. Start with a little hill, after you reach the bottom line pull the stroke up and leave a little tail. Then cross that stroke with a straight line from the upper right side to the lower left. Then start a new hill:

Now let's practice writing the letter 'x' separately. Start with a little hill, after you reach the bottom line pull the stroke up and leave a little tail. Then cross that stroke with a straight line from the upper right side to the lower left:

Lesson 23: Words with letters 'z', 'v' and 'x'

In this lesson you will practice writing words using letters and strokes that you've learnt so far. Practice writing these words until you'll get comfortable writing them:

wizard wizard wizard

wizard wizard wizard

sanny sanny sanny

sanny sanny sanny

crazy crazy crazy

crazy crazy crazy

Lesson 24: Long curved wave stroke

In this lesson you will learn how to write a long curved wave stroke. It is similar to the short curved stroke that you've learnt only it reaches the top line:

Lesson 25: Uppercase letters 'C', 'A' and 'O'

In this lesson you will learn how to write uppercase letters 'C', 'A' and 'O'. These letters look very similar to their lowercase counterparts. Let's start with the letter 'C'. Simply make a single long curved wave stroke:

Now let's continue with the letter 'A'. Start at the top line, make a curved wave stroke, touch the beginning of the stroke and then come back down:

Now we'll learn how to write the letter 'O'. Start at the top line, make a curved wave stroke, touch the beginning of the stroke, then make a little loop and pull the stroke to the right:

Lesson 26: Words with letters 'C', 'A' and 'O'

In this lesson you will practice writing words using letters and strokes that you've learnt so far. Practice writing these words until you'll get comfortable writing them:

Letter 'O' is unusual as it ends with a tail close to the top line. The loop that it ends with changes when you need to connect the uppercase 'O' with other lowercase letters. Let's practice writing some words with this type of connection:

48

Oregon Oregon Oregon

Oregon Oregon Oregon

Omaha Omaha Omaha

Omaha Omaha Omaha

Ozark Ozark Ozark

Ozark Ozark Ozark

Lesson 27: Long wave stroke

In Lesson 1 you've already practiced writing long wave strokes. There are a number of uppercase letters that you can write using that type of stroke too. But first let's revise writing the long wave stroke itself:

Lesson 28: Uppercase letters 'U', 'Y' and 'V'

In this lesson you will learn how to write uppercase letters 'U', 'Y' and 'V'. These letters look very similar to their lowercase counterparts. Let's start with the letter 'U'. Start with a little tail near the top line, make a long wave stroke and finish with a little tail:

Now let's practice writing the letter 'Y'. Start with a little tail near the top line, make a long wave stroke, pull the stroke down below the bottom line, make a loop to the left, cross the stroke at the bottom line and finish with a little tail:

Now let's practice writing the letter 'V'. Start with a little tail near the top line, make a long wave stroke and stop at the top line:

Lesson 29: Words with letters 'U', 'Y' and 'V'

In this lesson you will practice writing words using letters and strokes that you've learnt so far. Practice writing these words until you'll get comfortable writing them:

Ukiah Ukiah Ukiah

Ukiah Ukiah Ukiah

Yonkers Yonkers Yonkers

Yonkers Yonkers Yonkers

Letter 'V' is unusual as it ends at the top line. To connect it with lowercase letters we will have to introduce a loop just like we did with the letter 'O' before. Let's practice writing some words with this type of connection:

Vancouver Vancouver

Vancouver Vancouver

Virginia Virginia

Virginia Virginia

Venice Venice Venice

Venice Venice Venice

Lesson 30: Uppercase letters 'T', 'F' and 'S'

In this lesson you will learn how to write uppercase letters 'T', 'F' and 'S'. Let's start with the letter 'T'. It consists of two strokes. Start close to the top line and make a vertical stroke to the bottom line, pull it to the left and make a little hook. Then make a wavy stroke on the top of the vertical stroke:

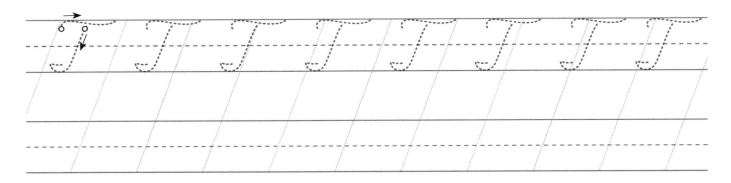

Now let's practice writing the letter 'F'. It consists of three strokes. Start close to the top line and make a vertical stroke to the bottom line, pull it to the left and make a little hook. Then make a wavy stroke on the top of the vertical stroke. Then make a small horizontal stroke at the middle line:

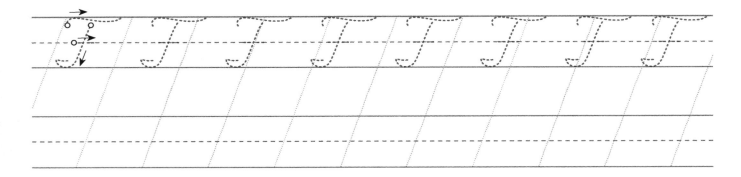

Now let's practice writing the letter 'S. It is a one-stroke letter. Start at the bottom line, curve up to the top line, make a loop that crosses itself at the middle line, touch the bottom line, then curve to the left across the initial stroke and make a little hook:

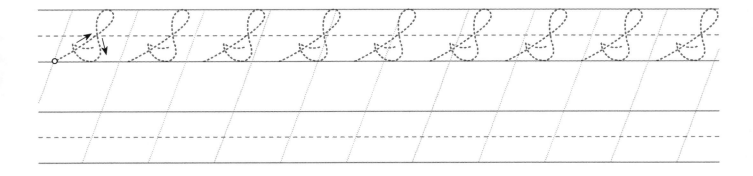

Lesson 31: Words with uppercase letters 'T', 'F' and 'S'

The common element of uppercase letters 'T', 'F' and 'S' is that little hook at the end. This hook is used to connect them to lowercase letters. Let's practice writing some words with this type of connection. Add horizontal strokes to 'T' and 'F' after you've written the whole word:

Tucson Tucson Tucson

Tucson Tucson Tucson

Fargo Fargo Fargo

Fargo Fargo Fargo

Salem Salem Salem

Salem Salem Salem

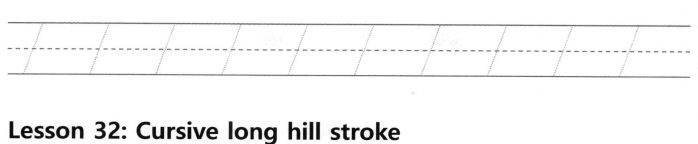

Lesson 32: Cursive long hill stroke

In this lesson we are going to practice the 'cursive long hill stroke'. It is similar to the cursive hill stroke that we've practiced before only the long one touches the top line:

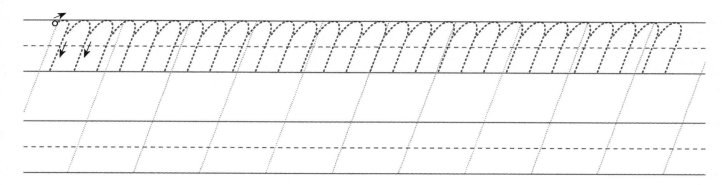

Lesson 33: Uppercase letters 'H', 'K', 'M' and 'N'

In this lesson you will learn how to write uppercase letters 'H', 'K', 'M' and 'N'. Let's start with the letter 'H'. This letter requires two strokes. Start with a small hook near the top line, then bring the stroke down to the bottom line. Then start the second stroke at the top line, bring it down to the bottom line, then make a loop that touches the first stroke and pull it to the right:

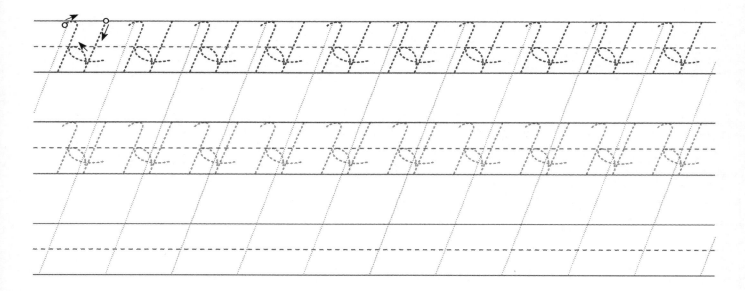

Now let's practice writing the letter 'K'. It consists of two strokes. Start with a small hook near the top line, then bring the stroke down to the bottom line. Then start the second stroke at the top line, pull it to the first stroke at the middle line, then pull it to the right with a little hook:

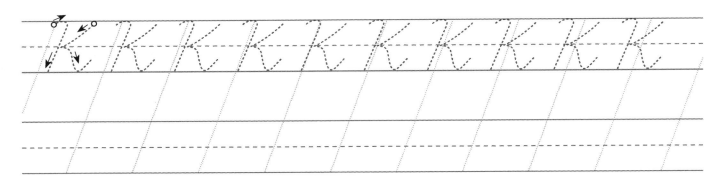

Now let's practice writing the letter 'M'. Start with small hook near the top line, make two long hill strokes and finish with a little tail:

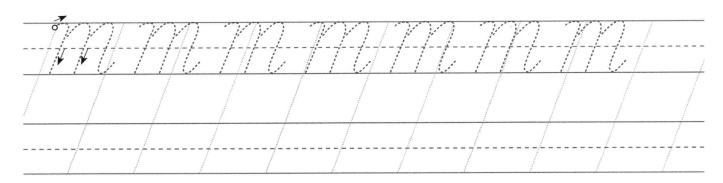

Now let's practice writing the letter 'N'. Start with small hook near the top line, make a long hill stroke and finish with a little tail:

Lesson 34: Words with uppercase letters 'H', 'K', 'M' and 'N'

In this lesson you will practice writing words using letters and strokes that you've learnt so far. Practice writing these words until you'll get comfortable writing them:

Newark Newark Newark

Newark Newark Newark

Hemet Hemet Hemet

Hemet Hemet Hemet

Kansas Kansas Kansas

Kansas Kansas Kansas

Miami Miami Miami

Miami Miami Miami

Norfolk Norfolk Norfolk

Norfolk Norfolk Norfolk

Hoover Hoover Hoover

Hoover Hoover Hoover

Lesson 35: Uppercase letters 'B', 'P', and 'R'

In this lesson you will learn how to write uppercase letters 'B', 'P', and 'R'. Let's start with the letter 'B'. Start with small hook near the top line, pull down to the bottom line, pull back along the same stroke, make a curve to the middle line, then another curve to the bottom line and finish with a little hook:

Now let's practice writing the letter 'P'. Start with small hook near the top line, pull down to the bottom line, pull back along the same stroke, make a curve just below the middle line:

Now let's practice writing the letter 'P'. Start with small hook near the top line, pull down to the bottom line, pull back along the same stroke, make a curve to the middle line, then pull the stroke to the right with an upward curve:

Lesson 36: Words with uppercase letters 'B', 'P', and 'R'

In this lesson you will practice writing words using letters and strokes that you've learnt so far. Pay attention to how uppercase letters connect the lowercase ones. Practice writing these words until they become easy to write:

Boston   Boston   Boston

Boston   Boston   Boston

Provo   Provo   Provo

Provo   Provo   Provo

Raleigh   Raleigh   Raleigh

Raleigh Raleigh Raleigh

Buffalo Buffalo Buffalo

Buffalo Buffalo Buffalo

Plano Plano Plano

Plano Plano Plano

Roswell Roswell Roswell

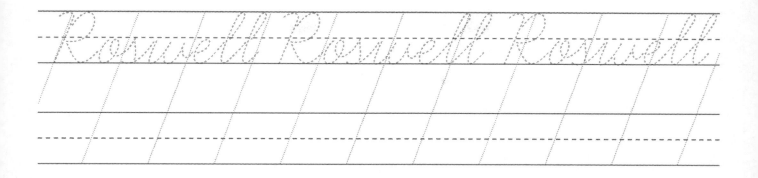

Lesson 37: Uppercase letters 'G', 'L', and 'Q'

In this lesson you will learn how to write uppercase letters 'G', 'L', and 'Q'. Let's start with the letter 'G'. Start with an upward curve, make a small loop below the top line, curve to the right, then pull down with a curve to the left and finish with a little hook:

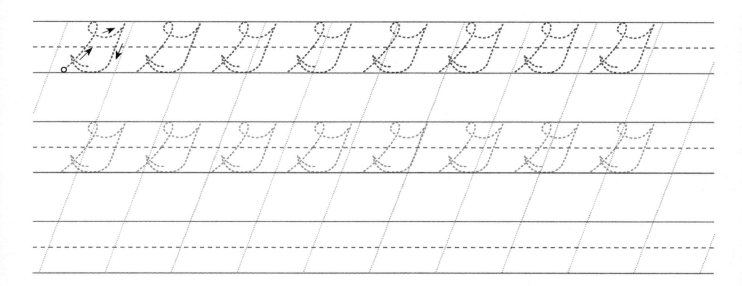

Now let's practice writing the letter 'L'. Start above the middle line, pull the curve to the right, make a small loop below the top line, then pull down and to the left, make a loop and finish with a little tail:

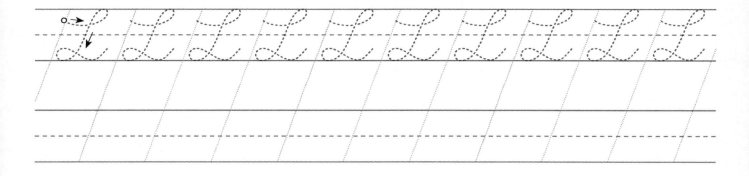

Now let's practice writing the letter 'Q'. Start slightly below the middle line, make a big arch that touches the top line, pull down and to the left to the bottom line, make a small loop and finish with a tail:

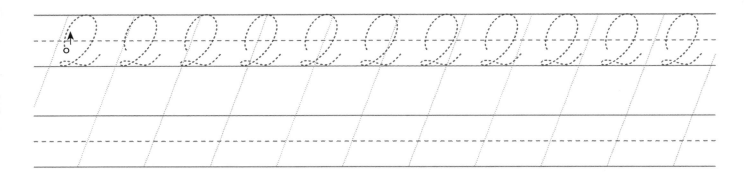

Lesson 38: Words with uppercase letters 'G', 'L', and 'Q'

In this lesson you will practice writing words using letters and strokes that you've learnt so far. Pay attention to how uppercase letters connect the lowercase ones. Practice writing these words until you'll get comfortable writing them:

Quincy Quincy Quincy

Quincy Quincy Quincy

Greeley Greeley Greeley

Greeley Greeley Greeley

Laredo Laredo Laredo

Laredo Laredo Laredo

Lesson 39: Uppercase letters 'D', 'E', and 'Z'

In this lesson you will learn how to write uppercase letters 'D', 'E', and 'Z'. Let's start with the letter 'D'. Start close to the top line, pull the stroke down, make a small loop to the left, then make a big curve to the right all the way to the top line and go slightly beyond:

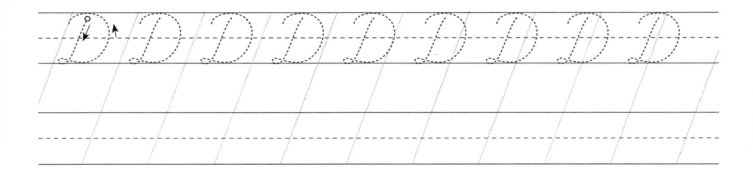

Now let's practice writing the letter 'E'. Start at the top line, curve down and to the left, make a little loop at the middle line, then curve down and to the left again:

68

Now let's practice writing the letter 'Z'. Start near the top line, make a curve that touches the top line and goes halfway between the middle and the bottom line, make a small loop there, curve down below the bottom line, make a loop there and finish with a tail:

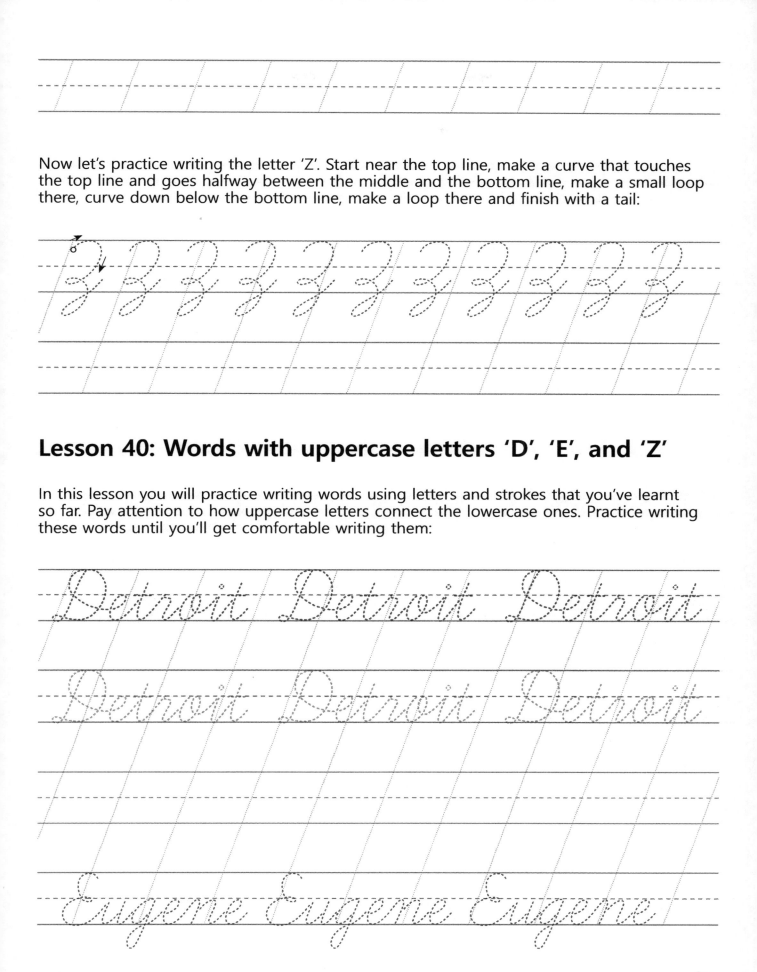

Lesson 40: Words with uppercase letters 'D', 'E', and 'Z'

In this lesson you will practice writing words using letters and strokes that you've learnt so far. Pay attention to how uppercase letters connect the lowercase ones. Practice writing these words until you'll get comfortable writing them:

Eugene Eugene Eugene

Zion Zion Zion Zion

Zion Zion Zion Zion

Dayton Dayton Dayton

Dayton Dayton Dayton

Eagan Eagan Eagan

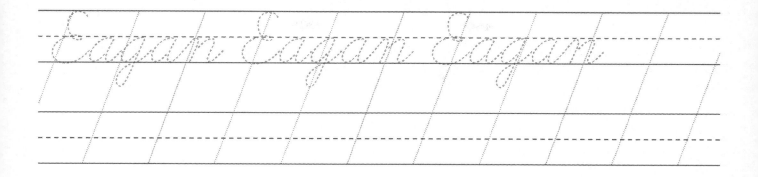

Lesson 41: Uppercase letters 'I' and 'J'

In this lesson you will learn how to write uppercase letters "I", and 'J'. Let's start with the letter 'I'. Start at the bottom line, pull the stroke up to the top line, make a big loop, then pull the stroke to the left and make a little hook:

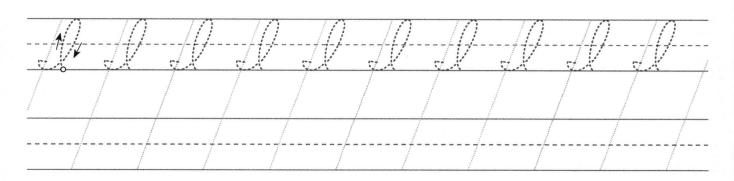

Now let's practice writing the letter 'J'. Start at the bottom line, pull up with a big curve that touches the top line, pull down below the bottom line, make a smaller curve there and finish with a little tail:

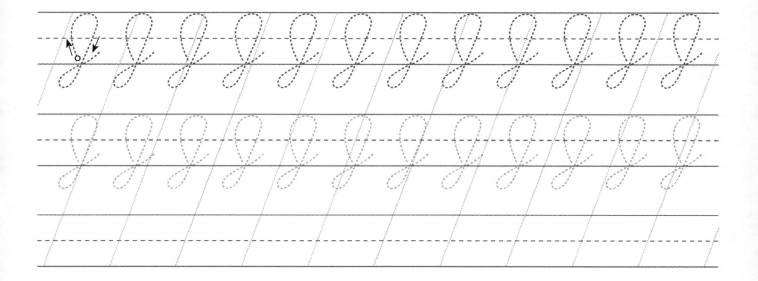

Lesson 42: Words with uppercase letters 'I' and 'J'

In this lesson you will practice writing words using letters and strokes that you've learnt so far. Pay attention to how uppercase letters connect the lowercase ones. Practice writing these words until they become easy to write:

Lesson 43: Uppercase letters 'W' and 'X'

In this lesson you will learn how to write uppercase letters "W", and 'X'. Let's start with the letter 'W'. Start with a small hook at the top line, pull down to the bottom line, then up with a little hook, then down again and then up again:

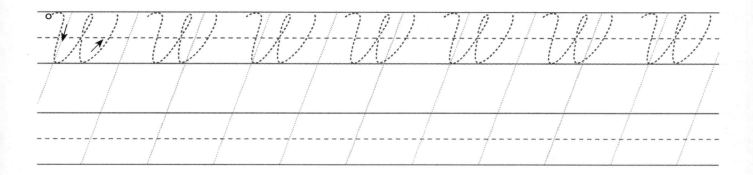

Now let's practice writing the letter 'X'. Start at the top line with a little hook, pull down and to the right, finish that stroke with a tail. Then cross the first stroke from top right to bottom left:

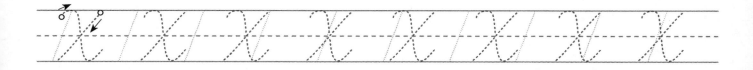

Lesson 44: Words with uppercase letters 'W' and 'X'

In this lesson you will practice writing words using letters and strokes that you've learnt so far. Pay attention to how uppercase letters connect the lowercase ones. Practice writing these words until they become easy to write:

Lesson 45: Numbers writing practice

Now that you've learned how to write all the uppercase and lowercase letters of the alphabet let's spend some time practicing writing numbers:

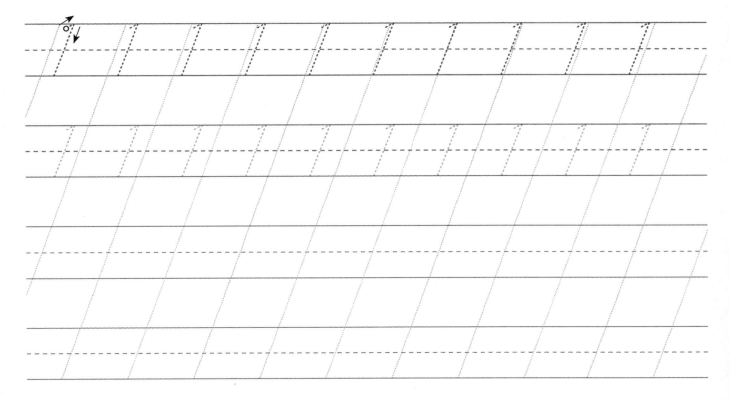

5 5 5 5 5 5 5 5 5

5 5 5 5 5 5 5 5 5

6 6 6 6 6 6 6 6 6

6 6 6 6 6 6 6 6 6

7 7 7 7 7 7 7 7 7

Lesson 46: Pangram writing practice

Congratulations! You have now mastered cursive handwriting of all the letters of the alphabet. To celebrate this let's practice writing some pangrams (sentences that contain all the letters of the alphabet).

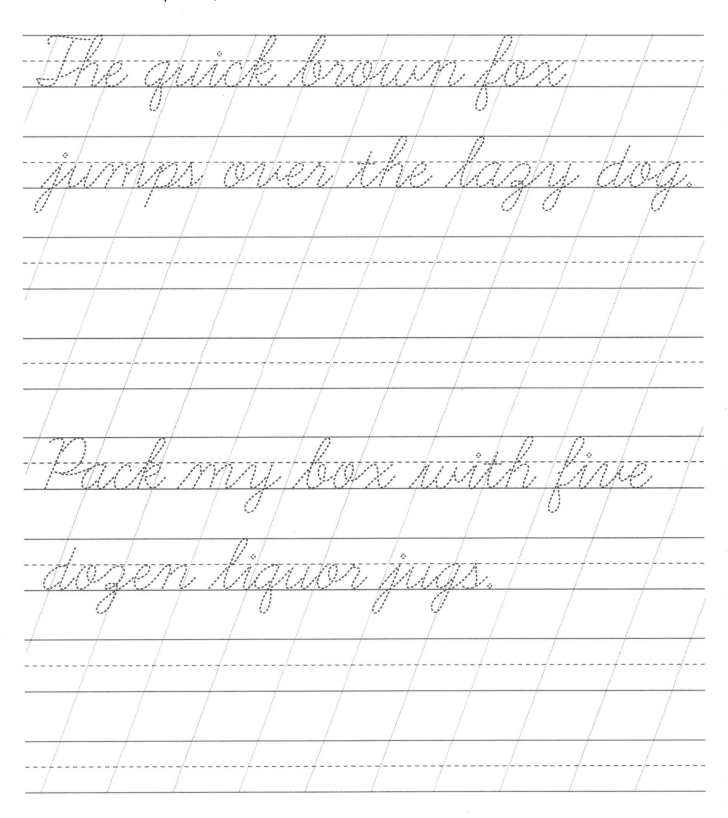

Jump by vow of quick

lazy strength in Oxford.

How quickly daft

jumping zebras vex.

Quick zephyrs blow,

vexing daft Jim.

Waltz, nymph, for

quick jigs vex bud.

Two driven jocks help

fax my big quiz.

Jackdaws love my big

sphinx of quartz.

Letters Writing Practice

A

Aa Aa Ab Ab Ac Ac

Ad Ad Ae Ae Af Af

Ag Ag Ah Ah Ai Ai

Aj Aj Ak Ak Al Al

Am Am An An Ao Ao

Ap Ap Aq Aq Ar Ar

As As At At Au Au

Av Av Aw Aw Ax Ax

Ay Ay Az Az

D

E

Ea Ea Eb Eb Ec Ec

Ed Ed Ee Ee Ef Ef

Eg Eg Eh Eh Ei Ei

Ej Ej Ek Ek El El

Em Em Em Em Eo Eo

Ep Ep Eq Eq Er Er

Es Es Et Et Eu Eu

Ew Ew Ew Ew Ex Ex

Ey Ey Ey Ey

G

H

I

Ha Ha Hb Hb Hc Hc
Hd Hd He He Hf Hf
Hg Hg Hh Hh Hi Hi
Hj Hj Hk Hk Hl Hl
Hm Hm Hn Hn Ho Ho
Hp Hp Hq Hq Hr Hr
Hs Hs Ht Ht Hu Hu
Hv Hv Hw Hw Hx Hx
Hy Hy Hz Hz

K

Na Na Nb Nb Nc Nc

Nd Nd Ne Ne Nf Nf

Ng Ng Nh Nh Ni Ni

Nj Nj Nk Nk Nl Nl

Nm Nm Nn Nn No No

Np Np Nq Nq Nr Nr

Ns Ns Nt Nt Nu Nu

Nv Nv Nw Nw Nx Nx

Ny Ny Nz Nz

O

Q

Qa Qa Qb Qb Qc Qc

Qd Qd Qe Qe Qf Qf

Qg Qg Qh Qh Qi Qi

Qj Qj Qk Qk Ql Ql

Qm Qm Qn Qn Qo Qo

Qp Qp Qq Qq Qr Qr

Qs Qs Qt Qt Qu Qu

Qw Qw Qx Qx Qx Qx

Qy Qy Qz Qz

Ra Ra Rb Rb Rc Rc

Rd Rd Re Re Rf Rf

Rg Rg Rh Rh Ri Ri

Rj Rj Rk Rk Rl Rl

Rm Rm Rn Rn Ro Ro

Rp Rp Rq Rq Rr Rr

Rs Rs Rt Rt Ru Ru

Rv Rv Rw Rw Rx Rx

Ry Ry Rz Rz

S

U

Ua Ua Ub Ub Uc Uc

Ud Ud Ue Ue Uf Uf

Ug Ug Uh Uh Ui Ui

Uj Uj Uk Uk Ul Ul

Um Um Un Un Uo Uo

Up Up Uq Uq Ur Ur

Us Us Ut Ut Uu Uu

Uv Uv Uw Uw Ux Ux

Uy Uy Uz Uz

V

Va Va Vb Vb Vc Vc

Vd Vd Ve Ve Vf Vg

Vg Vg Vh Vh Vi Vi

Vj Vj Vk Vk Vl Vl

Vm Vm Vn Vn Vo Vo

Vp Vp Vq Vq Vr Vr

Vs Vs Vt Vt Vu Vu

Vv Vv Vw Vw Vx Vx

Vy Vy Vz Vz

Y

Ya Ya Yb Yb Yc Yc

Yd Yd Ye Ye Yf Yf

Yg Yg Yh Yh Yi Yi

Yj Yj Yk Yk Yl Yl

Ym Ym Ym Ym Yo Yo

Yp Yp Yq Yq Yr Yr

Ys Ys Yt Yt Yu Yu

Yv Yv Yw Yw Yx Yx

Yy Yy Yz Yz

Alternative Capital Letters

A

Aa Aa Ab Ab Ac Ac

Ad Ad Ae Ae Af Af

Ag Ag Ah Ah Ai Ai

Aj Aj Ak Ak Al Al

Am Am An An Ao Ao

Ap Ap Aq Aq Ar Ar

As As At At Au Au

Av Av Aw Aw Ax Ax

Ay Ay Az Az

D

H

Ha Ha Hb Hb Hc Hc

Hd Hd He He Hf Hf

Hg Hg Hh Hh Hi Hi

Hj Hj Hk Hk Hl Hl

Hm Hm Hn Hn Ho Ho

Hp Hp Hq Hq Hr Hr

Hs Hs Ht Ht Hu Hu

Hw Hw Hw Hw Hx Hx

Hy Hy Hz Hz

F

117

I

Ia Ia Ib Ib Ic Ic

Id Id Ie Ie If If

Ig Ig Ih Ih Ii Ii

Ij Ij Ik Ik Il Il

Im Im In In Io Io

Ip Ip Iq Iq Ir Ir

Is Is It It Iu Iu

Iw Iw Iuu Iuu Ix Ix

Iy Iy Iz Iz

J

Sentences Writing Practice

Alan asks Amelia about

apricots.

Blair brought books on

bees to Bob.

Crystal cooks creamy
corn chowder.

David delivers delicious
donuts daily.

Elise eats eclairs and eggs
every day.

Florence finished first in
the frog race.

George gave Graham

green goggles.

Hannah has a hairy

hamster named Henry.

Irene ice skates with

Inessa in Illinois.

Jenny just ate John's

jelly beans from a jar.

Keira keeps her keys in
the kitchen.

Luke loves little lemurs
and lemmings.

Mason misses mountain
climbing in Montana.

Nolan's niece Nora needs
a new necklace.

Oscar owns the only

olive orchard in town.

Peter pretends preparing

for philosophy exam.

Quentin ate quite a bit of
quiche.

Robin reads books about
running rabbits.

Sean sees something
slithering in the sand.

Tobin tends to try new
things on Tuesdays.

Usher urges Uwe to get
under an umbrella.

Vincent visited Valerie
for vacation in Venice.

Winston wishes winters

were warmer.

Xavier xeroxed old

X-rays for Xenia.

Yuri eats yummy

yogurt and and yolks.

Zara zigzagged to the

zoo to see the zebras.

134

Blank Writing Practice Sheets